THE PORTAGE POETRY SERIES

I0530348

SERIES TITLES

Bowed As If Laden With Snow
Megan Wildhood

Silent Letter
Gail Hanlon

New Wilderness
Jenifer DeBellis

Fulgurite
Catherine Kyle

The Body Is Burden and Delight
Sharon White

Bone Country
Linda Nemec Foster

Not Just the Fire
R.B. Simon

Monarch
Heather Bourbeau

The Walk to Cefalù
Lynne Viti

The Found Object Imagines a Life: New and Selected Poems
Mary Catherine Harper

Naming the Ghost
Emily Hockaday

Mourning
Dokubo Melford Goodhead

Messengers of the Gods: New and Selected Poems
Kathryn Gahl

After the 8-Ball
Colleen Alles

Careful Cartography
Devon Bohm

Broken On the Wheel
Barbara Costas-Biggs

Sparks and Disperses
Cathleen Cohen

Holding My Selves Together: New and Selected Poems
Margaret Rozga

Lost and Found Departments
Heather Dubrow

Marginal Notes
Alfonso Brezmes

The Almost-Children
Cassondra Windwalker

Meditations of a Beast
Kristine Ong Muslim

PRAISE FOR

they were horrible cooks

"With honesty, humanity, and wit, *They Were Horrible Cooks* intermixes historical themes and everyday traumas, boldly laying bare the realities and ironies of a dog-eat-dog world."

—TIYA MILES
author of *All that She Carried*
National Book Award Winner

"A husband reads his dead wife's poems to a spare crowd, while cannibals go hungry with no one to invite to dinner. Whether bearing witness to the torment of a mother who drowns her own children, or to the quiet sorrows of daughters mourning their mother by fingering the thread of her old coats, Whittenberg never fails to illuminate crucial truths at the center of human experience. These poems cut to the bone and remind the reader of the infinitely tender agonies of being human."

—NOMI EVE
author of *Henna House*

"Allison Whittenberg embraces the topic of family though she's haunted by memories—in 'Truce' the father has been abusive, but he and the daughter bake a pumpkin pie together, and they're able to laugh at the 'neon orange mess.' And in 'Lag,' the mother's final words, 'Please return the library books,' become 'the sum of my mother.' Beyond family, Whittenberg gives us little jewels of poems, some exploring four strong women: Phillis Wheatley, Doris Rivkina, Hedy Lamarr, and Vivian Dandridge. There are many lovely poems here that I savored—one of my favorites is in the voice of a firefly: 'I can't mate with the lights on.'"

—KAREN LOEB
author of *Jump Rope Queen*

"Allison Whittenberg's *They Were Horrible Cooks* is a delight to discover, and then read over and over, savoring each line. The poems approach minimalism without being postmodern about it; they use spare construction to depict common situations with a sharp wit, wasting no extra time on descriptive details. There is pain in many of these emotional snapshots, but there is also joy. Even the book's title, which is not the title of a poem in it, but a poem's last line, takes a situation of incest abuse and gives a surprise humorous twist to it. There is proverbial wisdom here—'(Rebellions are revolutions that didn't work)'—observations that make trite phrases resonate with irony—'Fun was had, or, / at least, impersonated'—and her poems' endings are like the description of death in 'Death'—'like the ending / of a good miniseries / surprising…/inevitable…' There are historical issues like a reference to Phillis Wheatley, touched upon lightly, and a surprising application, in 'slavery,' to the poet's life in frustrated expectation. This is a collection that reads easily and rewards rereading often."

—DON RIGGS
author of *Bilateral Asymmetry*

they
were
horrible
cooks

poems

allison whittenberg

CORNERSTONE PRESS
UNIVERSITY OF WISCONSIN-STEVENS POINT

Cornerstone Press, Stevens Point, Wisconsin 54481
Copyright © 2024 Allison Whittenberg
www.uwsp.edu/cornerstone

Printed in the United States of America by
Point Print and Design Studio, Stevens Point, Wisconsin

Library of Congress Control Number: 2024940025
ISBN: 978-1-960329-56-1

All rights reserved.

Cornerstone Press titles are produced in courses and internships offered by the
Department of English at the University of Wisconsin–Stevens Point.

DIRECTOR & PUBLISHER
Dr. Ross K. Tangedal

EXECUTIVE EDITORS
Jeff Snowbarger, Freesia McKee

EDITORIAL DIRECTOR
Ellie Atkinson

SENIOR EDITORS
Brett Hill, Grace Dahl

PRESS STAFF
Carolyn Czerwinski, Allison Lange, Sophie McPherson, Kylie Newton, Natalie
Reiter, Ava Willett, Cam Williams

to the words that feed us

ALSO BY ALLISON WHITTENBERG:

Maine Under Water

Sane Asylum

Carnival of Reality

Tutored

Sweet Thang

Hollywood and Maine

Life Is Fine

CONTENTS

they
were
horrible
cooks

Words Leave Me Hungry

What do cannibals do about dinner
when there is nobody around?
I remember the first time I had sex, only because every
other time was better
Do all journeys last forever?
I don't write much anymore
just a line or two
per year
If the past is deep,
is the future shallow?
They don't come,
the visions
All I see is nothing
And more nothing
It's not like when I was young and throbbing beneath
that body so much larger than mine everything was
bigger than me back then
bigger, bolder
There is no substitute for human contact.

here, at the barnes and borders

an ambulance was parked outside
crisis? no
the emts were inside—browsing
at that barnes and borders
a dark-haired girl band was testing,
testing 1, 2
testing for 20 minutes
testing then
strumming acoustics sourly
a gray-haired man at a far table clapped
other patrons ignored the mandatory ambiance thumb-
ing through, cackling
over us weakly or merely chatting
it's such, such a great place to chat
in the noble borders, a store that serves
chai and dvds
muffins and cds
anything you please
you can buy a necklace there
the assistant manager has a degree from nyu
it's in english
she swears she'll use that degree, someday

Our Plight

In some countries,
Poets are persecuted: jailed,

Beaten, even hung
In America, they have it harder;

Here,
we ignore them.

Synchronizing

I'm indigent, I think
And you are poignant
In my heart, like an instrument
Are you there to pierce
Or to mend?

Doppelganger emotions
With their fervid, florid intentions

Clutching happiness by its throat
How does the theorem add?
One plus one
So simple to apprehend, yet so hard I never know if I'm
fighting
For peace or merely reposing
Between battles
What did Wilde say,

Who, in love, is poor?
Whoever has love is rich?

There is a difference.

Applying for Amnesty

My love is diabolical
Incendiary as the concept: Freedom

                              And just as elusive
Will it be liberty or death?
Die in my arms?
Die.
Prove your sincerity
Go without something vital

                              Like liquid
You'll find my "intensions" clear,
Clear as running water
                    And soft, soft as melting snow

I need an angel to be angel-like to me but not

Angelic, you know
I need your hands on me,
              except when I don't need your hands on me

I need to feel semi-special
(except when I want to be independent)

My fibrous heart is just porous enough
to kind of let you in part way

I lust you.
              Do you lust me?

Loop

in your life,
you will have something that you cherish
and you will nurture it,
tend to it,
love it,
call it *beautiful*
because you made it; *beautiful*
that's human nature

in that same life,
some people will come, along
destroy what you made,
rip it,
tear it,
crush it,
stomp on it,
mar it,
turn it ugly...

because that's human nature

Sustainable

eating eggshells
for calcium—
crushed to mush,
watered down.
is this the future
we pray for?
wanting not to waste,
as waste fills our needs

Did you know?

Eggshells are painted white
for uniformity?
for aesthetics?
for supremacy!
(even the produce section at Acme is against diversity...)

In the Nick

Progress in the process
Crews toiling with blizzard speed
Monkeying between branches
Risking life to cut limbs

Stumped

Lumbered

Why the rush?

What if the ominous omnibus
Missed?

The Conflict, Plus Six Months

each night,
the moon had the company of stars...
yet you, in basic,
inoculated against
1,000 afflictions,
are back
safe
(not one of the alphabetized listed dead, as remembered
as frogs)
but missing
something
nonetheless
free to
acclimate to
the reality
of camouflage
illusions
     naked
          without being heard
     lost
          without being held
     blind,
     metaphorically,
          without being fed
this need leads to invisible
disease till
you have 50 years
left,
     plus the conflicts

A Husband's Duty

Next poem
Facts shifts sometimes
She passed away three years ago
        after being sick for two and a half years.
She passed away two and a half years ago
        after being sick for three years.

Uncomfortable, he laughs then clears his throat
He is reading his dead wife's poetry
To a spare conference crowd
She wasn't a headliner in life either.

Next poem
He had videos of her reading,
why didn't he just play them?
Save himself all this

Getting into a gray suit
trying to match her cadence
keeping a brave, yet empathetic face

Next poem
Words about the birth of their twins,
Words about the moving from Connecticut,
Words about the words not coming

Next poem
Words about animals, pottery, dance
Words about wounds

"If anyone would like to take a look at her books or purchase"
        he told the gathering
"Do you take a check?" someone interrupted

That Uninvited Guest

loneliness,
my companion
as I stay in
or go out
people ask, "are you here, alone?"
yes, I am, but I brought alone with me
to sit
with
and
not talk to

Salt, Thorns, Otis Redding, Why?

Salt without bread

Thorns on a cactus

Otis Redding, I miss you

Why didn't you go Greyhound?

Eat the Indians First

Them: (The Donner Party)
Go west, young man, and get lost
In this coldest winter in California's history
Eye two Indians as scouts, then
As dinner
The savages won't eat human flesh, even if it dies
From natural causes
Ironically, the Christians had no such restrictions
When the going gets tough,
The braves get eaten.

Us: (The two Indians)
Another day, outgunned
They said we stole their cattle
We should have stayed in our wigwam
We were only trying to help
One by one, they dropped because they didn't
Pack right
Till an epiphany comes
Why... not... eat... the...
When they decided, we take that long walk
Toward eternity
And really what does it matter?
They have taken our land, our women and children.
What is left then to be eaten down to the bone.

Extant

shame on you

for eating flesh

the protein of your friends

(at least, you didn't eat your sister)

but come on-what were you thinking?

to maintain

survival excuses everything except when it doesn't shame

after your plane crashed into the andes mountains after
the impact, the crush of metal, the raging fire drowned
by the snow

more bad luck

the avalanche, the avalanches

being lost, being broken

and you can't eat the rugby balls and the plane food is
gone. the hunger, the relentless cold, the hunger, the
screams, where was the utility?

civilization sent search parties that couldn't find you shame

nourishment was only a 60 mile walk away or at least
the goat herders

you had to find your own cure

you saved yourself

shame

Watching Jordan's Fall

… God, I hate November
All the hope I had hoped
Against hope for Jordan.

Dad beat Jordan, to
Straighten him out, to show
Jordan, to silence him.

My brother lived until the next
Season, onto the next winter,
Voiceless, like a fallen leaf.

Poets Cry

in pittsburgh, the hill district, it was never dire
tight, yes
scraping by with trolley car rides
crosstown
then again crosstown
saturday entertainment
all day
 mama held my hand, reassured
 I learned love

Lag

You realize,
Please return the library books
They're on the table
Were her last words
Returning the loan out of every *I love you* she'd given

Instead of goodbye
The incessant familiarity of instruction
The sum
$\qquad\qquad\qquad\qquad$ of my mother

Season's Denial

The first year it happened I wondered if I would outgrow dreaming of the dead by night and going through the motions of duty by day? The eggnog circulated, and I know what an egg is, but what is nog? Fun was had, or, at least, impersonated. It's Christmas, for Christ's sake.

Ribbons undone…

Gifts swapped…

Turkey knifed – someone's absent.

She's cited briefly during grace, but only then: This day is about sugar plum fairies, not protoplasm.

Truce

For the girl abused by her father,
The terrible is the beautiful
In between, he showed range
Embracing a new word from the family dictionary:
Fun

A pumpkin nearly half her size that he let her pick

They came home from the patch and clawed out its guts

He put the face in the window
Without a recipe, they baked happiness
On that stunted, gray afternoon
A can of condensed milk and molasses

The outside, cold as reality
Inside, warm. Warm as television

They laughed when the pie turned out to be
A horrid tasting neon orange mess
Because that day, they were not tragic figures;
They were horrible cooks.

Losing Religion

I'm through
        with sunsets!
I'm through
        with sex!
I'm through
        with life!

(he confessed in his still potent
voice while in his starving blue gown
on the sixth floor of Mercy Fitzgerald
daughter propped him walking his cemented
joints unsure if his articulations
were dizzy delirium or final clarity
mother had been gone,
going on a decade
daughter couldn't recall him being in circulation
what congress was he referring to
always going into the hospital for the last time hitting the rafters
with histrionics about
his peter and the gold of sunsets
and titillating
existentialism.)

Coats

When my mother was young, she was rich

So rich that her father bought her a coat

Straight from a well-known department store

At ten after closing
Time by knocking on the window
And shaking a hand full of money at the manager.
It was a prepossessing coat.
Georgia-clay-red with a furry collar.
When my mother got a little older, her family was poor
And her mother and her had to share a coat.
One had to wait for the other to come in, order to go out.
It was a hideous coat.
Dull black like something a pallbearer would wear.
When she passed away,
My sister and I quarrel over her belongings
One coat, particularly.
It was chic
Camel-colored, cinching at the waist.
My father threw salt,
Saying it looked better on me
Through persistence, I won it.
She was a disguised, mostly silent woman.
What I know of my mother, I glean from thread.

The Circumstances

The man whipping my double latte
Has a deep knife scar
Across his throat
Whoever got him, got him good
I wonder…
Was he victim or victimizer?
There's a stereotype for each scenario

Was it one of those mismatched fights—
Fist to switchblade? Did he welch on a deal?

Does he have a bad-ass girlfriend?
Could it be from a jealous ex?
Accidental. Was it?

Had he done time?
Is earning six-fifty an hour

Making four-dollar

Cups of coffee

Getting on the right track?

Day Job

After a night of therapeutic bottle and blunt passing

He wakes on earth at 5a.m.

In a lumpy bed
He goes to the airport in his overalls
Brandishing a handkerchief
He scrubs the thick plastic windows
With long handles and bruises
He watches the jets take off
They move hot through the endless sky
With purpose

Days and Dollars

tan uniformed security guard waits

behind his own kind of prison

the grind of his 10-7 gig

eyeballing shoppers, separating buyers from the
browsers and boosters

what does it mean? what does anything mean?

as the frail flexible gray bars clack open

for opening

How we sat on opposite sides of the room after
fuckingsexmakinglove or however you want to
look at it

How you didn't kiss me before leaving
How I didn't want you to
How funny life is
How long it's been
How many weeks
How out of practice you were
How late it had gotten
How long we've known each other
How little we know about each other
How do you know when the next earthquake will strike
And how come?

YouTube Sucks

what does the fix feed?
our emptiness,

all those crevices, those vacancies

we have a right to be ill-informed

so we can act like we're acting

past lies
present lies
future malformations

we keep needing to do something
time gallops and escapes
as we mine the hours

never tasting the nectar

just feeling the squeeze

Water's Wine

The balance of bliss is pain
The balance of pain is enlightenment
The balance of enlightenment is more enlightenment
The balance of more enlightenment is transcendence
The balance of transcendence is alienation
The balance of alienation is bliss

Mice and Men

there are guys
whose rippling impression
vanishes like a paddle upon water
dance partners, set ups,
and weirdos as forgotten
as canceled magazine subscriptions

animals fare better
marvel at the house mouse
unforgettable, as he flees your wrath
65 mph, he's history now

God gave him the skills to cope, to live
in your mind, burrow under your skin
he's a gray blur of freedom from you
so independent, yet living off crumbs
each night, you wonder
where is he?

Quilt

slaves recognize the metaphor
putting odds together with ends
knitting scraps into sturdy shape

manipulating fabric
irregular shapes
functional, enduring

making a way
out of no way

Two Memories

You slammed me against the wall
and shook me
but I fought you off
my 106 pounds to your 270
I fought
I don't remember what I said to you to make you go off
I never got used to the eggshell walk
I'm not good at bathing men's egos
you were always bigger/older
doing things before me then
I started doing things before you
I was just back from college for Thanksgiving break
full of ideas
working your nerves
that's the last time you touched me

The first time you touched me
I was playing in your room
I broke your toy, sorry, memorabilia.
you came home from school and saw the mess of paste patchwork
connecting the disconnected plastic
I looked into your eyes, black eyes
you told me you weren't mad
you knew that I tried...

Race Theory

In day, color
Like sweat or smoke
Rise above like mercury, precluding
The face: unimportant

Turning 30

Lately,

I've fallen

Completely

In love with myself

When I look in the mirror

A sense of self-esteem

Courses through me and all I can think of is "Damn, If you ain't fine."

Vivian Seeks Stardom

when your pretty face is pretty
but not otherworldly pretty as your sister's
when you married at least five times
when your sultry singing and body wiggling
caused no seismic shift
when being black royalty wasn't enough
when you disappear into France
and a private eye finds you
when the highlight of your career
is starring in *Coal Black and Da Sebban Dwarfs*
(and that was voice work)

(even Dorothy couldn't win an Oscar,
and she had everything,
ev-er-y-thing Hollywood wanted,
except ...)

it all boiled down to the *when* (the golden age)
the *when* is the *why*
it's *how* hard you tried
as if some day
it would all fall into place.

The condition of alienation

Life is a bread factory,
constantly
pressing out more of the same.
There was a time when I
sidestepped the man
with the crazy laugh, but now,
he's intriguing, as a mirror.
On Animal Planet, thirty lion cubs band together
to take down one elephant.
Have you ever felt sorry for an elephant,
or a crazy man,
or
bread?

Dora Circa the War Years

For remembrance, the picture of her girlish dark-haired
freshness and a taut, three-paragraph bio was posted on
a flagpole

For a week, students passed her, too wrapped up in
their own bad days and stressors, their own crosses to
bear, to notice

Hiding, maneuvering,
creating a bottomless sense of chaos
Dora had spent her wonder years as a partisan
making makeshift weapons out of lost parts
seeping in forests
using her trusty machine gun as a pillow
evading, plotting,
breathing almost to the date of liberation
She had escaped the ghettos,
the train rides, the liquidations
until too many Germans surrounded,
demanding they produce a Jew
disarmed, momentary solidarity melted to basic instinct
someone pointed out Dora.
They bound her hands
tied a rock to her neck
threw her in the river
then shot her twice

An empty, gray ending to a would have been
full, green life
Under other circumstances

Death,

you greedy motherfucker
seems like
you're always around
                    harvesting
with your miscarriages
lurking defects
lingering complications
accidents
and the light
the way you up and leave
everything
unfinished
like the ending
of a good miniseries
surprising...
inevitable...

Three Acts

my children drowned
16 months ago
2 years ago
6 years ago

my children, just as naked,
as now, just as submerged back when
we moved through the uncertainty of shelters,
sustained by government crumbs,
their father not my husband.

the voices talk
pharmaceutical extractions mute
the voices shout

are there sharks under the golden gate?

i drive to the bridge
God is there, but he blinks
i strip my babies and listen to the smell of the bay
it fills me, the soft rays
illuminate

i do it.
again.
once more.

in your news reports, please include the following:
i'm drowning too.

My Vocation

I assumed
you knew
it was busy work
–that journal I assigned–
where you poured out
the turn of events, your plans, and suicidal tendencies

I didn't realize high school was HIGH SCHOOL

Seasoned, I went through the motions and didn't invest

It's too late
to read you now…

Sorry
Sorry means nothing
Goodbye and sorry all the same

… and, Joan Crawford left her daughter

nothing
in her will,

not even
        a wire hanger.

Phillis

Call her a servant, rather than a slave
Have her versify our beauty, our God, our civilization
Have her vilify her motherland
During the trial, John Hancock asked,
"Can she think for herself?"
"No" Master Wheatley replied,
"But she can think."

Hedy

beauty,
the curse
that coursed
through her
aggressively
how dare
she have a brain
under
such a face
all this was said to be so...unfortunate
pretty and smart?
unfortunate?
that's a joke–
right?

slavery

life sucks
in spots
where
you hope
things will
get better
in between these
day-by-day, days by days
you get older
and older
and you keep
answering
"I'm fine"
like
you
mean
it

F. Scott

in *Esquire*, he compares himself to
a lion?
no,
an eagle?
no,
a cracked plate...

a   cracked   plate

a cracked plate...
too fragile for detergent
too fragile to shuffle with other dishes

what did he know,
he was only a writer

You Made My Life a Living Hell

And I love you.
Oh, oh, how I treasure our recreational arguments,
the yellow worms of our pettiness. Our
chemistry is our friction. Your benignly
lacerating tongue. The octopus-like suction cups
of your attention. How can I live without
you? How can I live without wishing
every day I'd never met you?
How can I forget to forget to remember
that when you're not here to work this shit out of me
it's just a drag.

Over 40, Finding, in America, a Guy

They don't want brown bananas
They want barely legal lime green ones
falling from the vine
They catch and *carpe diem* them

Tarry, Miss Setting Sun, scratch like a chicken
Scratches the soil for worms (eligible bachelors
or anything, breathing)

Your rebellion was televised (on HBO)
Are you a Charlotte
or a Miranda?
(Rebellions are revolutions that didn't work)

You stayed at the carnival merely long enough to win a stigma

Did you really have to get a PhD
in chemistry?
And Miss Rice, did you really have to learn six foreign languages?
A man should have your job
He has families to support,
(the old one he left behind
and the young one he's just begun)

Take

the truth from
the story to create
the myth that becomes
the history that is taken for truth
that we die for

Critical

In the absence of panic
I spy the obscene waste of time.
The plane flames, crashing
Found footage streams the frantic
Seemingly endless waste of words: rushed garbled mangled
From everybody lucky enough to get to a cell
State the obvious:
It's the end; I've reached you; I love you; duh

Deal

Mr. Pancake's esse was flat
till he met a woman who was sweet,
fondant

For a while, she made his life
interesting
riveting, as sugar granules poured down his throat
abrasive,
exciting,
too diabetically rich.

He considered avoidance, returning to the regular
dreich,
he pretended she didn't exist
but, in times of hollowness, Mr. Pancake

Waffled.

lucency

amongst a breathless,
debilitating,
incapacitating,
panic attack
i
told
myself
not to panic

and...

without warning
i
was
suddenly
all
right.

Life slips

like two weeks like five years like coupon clippings
from a thick Sunday pull out
shiny, vivid
promising bargains in primary colors
$4 off a $40 or more purchase! EXPIRED
$1 off cotton balls, swabs and rounds EXPIRED
20% of not tomorrow or yesterday
today and today only

Life as a Cliché

So trite, my boss, stereotypically balding, puts his hands on my shoulder while I process words instead of word processing. Are you some kind of writer? he asks. When I don't answer, his hands move up to play with my earrings, which dangle parallel my cheekbones. Can you work late tonight? He wants to know.

So I had to fuck him. Certainly, I can't support myself off my anemic symbolism, my flabby free verse. I need to keep my clerical skills employed.

The next morning, during dictation, in my embroidered white blouse, crisp to the point of snapping, I remain unaltered. Our eyes meet: his loaded with metaphor; mine without the least suggestion of allusion.

Regrets?

Shake me
Kiss me
Make me
Give in

Ignore my innocence
Appeal to my curiosity

Leave me to my

uncertainty

In a few weeks
I'll worry about reputation, AIDS, pregnancy

In a few years
I'll worry about self-esteem.

I can't mate with the lights on

said the firefly
(endangered)
artificial light has been hacking my groove since Edison
it's getting harder and harder to find tall grass man
I'm about to flicker out

me and the glowworms
it's lights out at our larval stage

we like it hot and humid
we need it hot and humid and dark

so have a heart
                    set the mood
                              and kill the lights

Vainglorious

they say: it's better to be alone
than to be in crowd of selfish people

exception

if you're Jay Gatsby
and that's the very thing that made you
Great...

One World Or None

Mama, how come you never told me about the A-
bomb?

Were we too busy
running from the men
with pillowcases and sheets
to duck and cover?

How come there's never
any of us in those
public service announcements?

They claim we can't get
a suntan, but are we also
immune to gamma rays?

Is it like flesh-colored
crayons, something that
was created without
us in mind?

There weren't
whites only signs
on the air raid shelters
so I guess
they would
have
cracked
open
the door,
if we knocked
hard enough,
right?

We would have been
one
big
happy family
at the end of the world,
wouldn't we?

The Black Writer

cold black words
corrupt the pale
virginity of paper
changing innocence
dark transforms it from
eden, with tiny letters
that mean something,
with quick hands, you
peck the nothingness
because you are inclined to tell the world
what's on your mind ruining the blank
chastity of empty whiteness.

Temperate

my dry wit
held its own
as the rain came down
in spits
then a geyser
we kept talking and talking at the outside table
al fresco all wet, oh
still
your zingers
priceless
in the dampness
left us
talking about every little
everything
every
thing.

ACKNOWLEDGMENTS

Indebted acknowledgement is made to the editors of the following publications in which these poems, in some form, first appeared:

"Coats": *BMA: The Sonia Sanchez Review*

"Death,": *But You Don't Look Sick*

"Words Leave Me Hungry": *Rockhurst Review*

"Here at the Barnes and Borders": *Wisconsin Academy Review*

"Our Plight": *Gargoyle*

"Synchronizing": *Dreich*

"The Conflict, Plus Six Months": *Vilas Avenue*

"Salt, Thorns, Otis Redding, Why?": *Isles of Mist Review*

"Watching Jordan's Fall": *Kaleidoscope: Exploring the Experience of Disablity through Literature and Fine Arts*

"Lag": *Poetry Wales*

"Truce": *J Journal*

"Losing Religion": *Spiky Palms*

"Condition of Alienation": *300 Days of Sun*

"The Circumstances": *Imitation Fruit*

"Day Job": *Riversedge*

"how we sat on opposite sides of after fuckingsexmakinglove or whatever however you want to look at it": *Red Owl*

"Water's Wine": *Judd's Hill Poetry Collection*

"Mice and Men": *Loud Voices Silent Streets*

"Quilt": *US 1*

"Turning 30": *Redivider*

"Dora Circa the War Years": *Line of Advance*

"Three Acts": *Phantom Kangaroo*

"Hedy" & "Lip Service": *Please See Me*

"Take": *86 Logic*

"Critical": *Vasant*

"Lucency": *New Orleans Review*

"Life slips": *The Blotter*

"Life as a Cliche": *Open: Journal of Arts and Letters*

"Regrets?": *Minyan*

"One World or None": *Gutter: The Magazine of New Scottish Writing*

"Race Theory": *De la Mancha: Step Out*

"Temperate": *Ability Maine: Breath and Shadow*

My thanks to Dr. Ross Tangedal, for plucking *They Were Horrible Cooks* out of the slush pile and putting me into the caring hands of amazing editors Grace Dahl and Kylie Newton. Thanks also to Ellie Atkinson, Brett Hill, and everyone at Cornerstone Press.

Special thanks to Marlowe for your nimble brain, your endless patience, and your quiet strength.

ALLISON WHITTENBERG is a Philadelphia native and the author of several books for young adults, including *Maine Under Water* (2024), *Tutored* (2010), *Hollywood and Maine* (2009), *Life Is Fine* (2007), and *Sweet Thang* (2006). Her poetry has been published widely in *Redivider, New Orleans Review, Columbia Review, Feminist Studies,* and elsewhere.

www.ingramcontent.com/pod-product-compliance
Lightning Source LLC
Chambersburg PA
CBHW031249120626
46545CB00007B/2716